Dreams to Reality

Turning Aspirations into Achievements, A Practical Guide to Transforming Dreams into Tangible Reality"

Donna Gray

Table of Contents

INTRODUCTION

Welcome to Dreams to Reality: Turning Aspirations into Achievements: A Practical Guide to Transforming Dreams into Tangible Reality. This book is designed to provide you with the tools, motivation, and inspiration you need to reach your highest potential. I believe that with the right mindset, anything is possible.

Through this book, I will help you to identify and unlock the secrets of success that are within you. You'll learn how to set powerful goals, develop a positive attitude, and take action to achieve them. I'll also provide you with the necessary strategies and techniques to stay motivated and overcome any obstacles that may arise. With the knowledge and skills gained from this book, you will be able to reach your goals and experience the success you deserve. So let's get to hear the story of Nina.

Nina was an ambitious young woman who had big dreams of becoming successful. She was determined to reach her goals, but she wasn't sure how to go about it. She had heard success stories of others, but she didn't know how to replicate it for herself.

Then one day, she came across the draft of my book called "Dreams to Reality: Turning Aspirations into Achievements, A Practical Guide to Transforming Dreams into Tangible Reality". She was intrigued and decided to give it a try. The book gave her an abundance of useful advice and tips that she could apply in her life. She learnt the importance of setting goals and having a plan to achieve them. She learnt how to stay motivated and focused on her dreams. She also learnt the importance of time management and making the most of every day.

Armed with a newfound sense of confidence, Nina started to make changes to her lifestyle. She began to set goals for herself and worked hard to achieve them. She made sure to set aside time each day for her own personal development. Over time, Nina began to see her dreams become a reality. She started to see the fruits of her labor and was filled with joy. She was now living the life she had always dreamed of and it was all thanks to the book she had read.

Nina is now a successful businesswoman, thanks to the wisdom she had gained from "Dreams to Reality: Turning Aspirations into Achievements, A Practical Guide to

Transforming Dreams into Tangible Reality" She was living proof that if you set your mind to something, you could make it happen.

I. UNDERSTANDING GOALS AND THE PATH TO SUCCESS

Understanding goals and the path to success are two of the most important aspects of achieving success in any endeavor. Goals provide direction and focus on what is important to the individual. By setting realistic goals, an individual can map out a path to success that is achievable and measurable.

The first step in understanding goals and the path to success is to identify what success looks like. This can be as simple as creating a list of achievable goals or as complex as setting long-term objectives. Once a goal is identified, it is important to create a plan that outlines the steps necessary to achieve that goal. This plan should include an assessment of the resources available, a timeline, and the steps that need to be taken to reach the desired outcome. Once a plan is in place, it is important to stay motivated and focused on the goal. This can be done by setting smaller, more achievable goals along the way.

It is also important to recognize successes and failures in order to keep track of progress. This will help to keep motivation high and will provide a sense of accomplishment. It is important to remember to stay flexible and open to change. As new opportunities or challenges arise, it may be necessary to adjust the plan. It is also important to remember that success is not always linear. It may take a few attempts to achieve a desired outcome, and that is okay.

Understanding goals and the path to success are essential to achieving success in any endeavor. By setting realistic goals and creating a plan to achieve them, an individual can stay motivated and focused on the goals. By remaining flexible and open to change, an individual can adjust the plan as necessary. With perseverance and dedication, success can be within reach.

A. DEFINING GOALS

A person or organization establishes goals when they are precise, quantifiable, and reachable objectives. There are three types of goals: short-, medium-, and long-term. Objectives may be broad or narrow. They may concern any aspect of life, including relationships, business, education, careers, health, and personal finances.

Aim for SMART goals, which stand for specific, measurable, achievable, relevant, and time-bound. Goal-setting and goal-achieving contribute to motivation, direction, focus, and a feeling of achievement.

B. UNDERSTANDING THE ROLE OF MINDSET

Mindset is an important factor in success and failure. It is the way we think and perceive things and is directly related to our attitudes, emotions, and behaviors. A person's mindset can be either fixed or growth-oriented.

A fixed mindset means that a person believes their abilities, talents, and intelligence are fixed traits that cannot be changed or improved. On the other hand, a growth mindset means that a person believes that their abilities, talents, and intelligence can be grown and developed over time. Having a growth mindset is important for personal and professional success.

People with a growth mindset tend to be more open to learning and trying new things, even when they make mistakes. They are also more likely to persist in the face of challenges and setbacks, because they believe in their ability to learn and grow from them. People with a fixed mindset, on the other hand, tend to be less motivated and may give up more easily when faced with challenges.

Understanding the role of mindset can help us make better decisions and take necessary steps to reach our goals. It is important to understand that our mindset can be changed, and that we can choose to adopt a growth mindset instead of a fixed mindset. By doing so, we can become more resilient.

Mindset is a set of beliefs, attitudes, and values that a person holds about themselves and their ability to succeed. It is a key factor in determining how successful a person will be in achieving their goals and reaching their full potential. People who have a positive mindset believe that they can achieve anything they set their minds to, while those who have a negative mindset may feel discouraged or unmotivated. The role of mindset is to give us the confidence to take on new challenges and reach our goals. It can also help us to stay focused and motivated.

If we believe we can succeed, we are more likely to take action and make progress. It also helps us to develop resilience and cope with failure. Having a positive mindset can help us in many areas of our lives, such as in our personal relationships, career, and education. It can help us to be more confident in our decisions and more open to taking risks. It can also help us to stay positive when faced with difficult circumstances.

In order to develop a positive mindset, it is important to be aware of our thoughts and beliefs and to challenge any negative beliefs we may have. It is also important to focus on our successes and to celebrate even small successes.

C. ESTABLISHING HABITS AND ROUTINES

Establishing habits and routines is key to achieving success in any area of life. Habits and routines help to reduce stress, save time, and increase productivity. They also help to reduce distractions and make it easier to stay focused on what is important.

The first step in developing habits and routines is determining your goals and priorities. Decide what you want to accomplish and then prioritize tasks accordingly. This will help you understand the habits and routines you'll need to develop to achieve your goals.

Next, make a timetable that works for you. This should contain a daily routine, a weekly schedule, and monthly goals. This will help you divide your goals into digestible portions, making it easier to plan and stay on track. Once you've identified your goals and created a schedule, you must adhere to it. Set reminders and reward yourself when you finish tasks.

Establishing habits and routines takes time, but it is worth the effort. With a little planning, consistency, and patience, you can create habits and routines that will help you reach your goals and lead to long term success.

III. STRATEGIES FOR REACHING YOUR GOALS

1. Set Clear Goals: Setting clear, achievable goals is the first step to reaching them. Be specific and realistic when setting your goals and make sure they are measurable.

2. Create a Plan: Once you have your goals set, create a plan of action to reach them. Break down the steps you need to take to achieve your goals and make sure you have a timeline for completing each step.

3. Track Your Progress: As you work towards your goals, be sure to track your progress. This will help you stay on track and motivated.

4. Get Support: Reaching your goals can be difficult and it's important to have a support system in place. Whether it's family, friends, or a support group, having people to cheer you on and help you can make all the difference.

5. Celebrate Your Successes: As you reach milestones along the way, be sure to take time to celebrate your successes. This will help you stay on track.

A. VISUALIZING AND AFFIRMING

Visualizing and affirming are two powerful tools for personal growth and development. Visualizing involves using the power of imagination to create a mental image of the desired outcome. Affirming involves repeating positive statements about oneself or the desired outcome to strengthen belief and motivation.

Together, these two techniques can be used to create a positive mindset and focus on achieving goals. Visualizing can help one to focus on their desired outcome and create a mental image of success. It is important to focus on the positive aspects of the goal and to be as detailed as possible when creating the mental image. This will help to create a positive and motivating environment.

Affirming can help to strengthen self-belief and motivation. Repeating positive statements helps to create a positive mindset and focus on achieving goals. It is important to be specific when creating affirmations and to believe in their power. Writing down affirmations and reading them aloud can help to reinforce the message and create a stronger connection with the desired outcome. When used together, visualizing and affirming can help to create a positive mindset and focus on achieving goals. They can be a powerful force for personal growth and development.

B. OVERCOMING OBSTACLES

Overcoming obstacles can be a difficult and daunting task, but it's important to remember that no matter how hard something may seem, it is possible to overcome any obstacle with dedication, hard work, and perseverance.

The key to overcoming obstacles is to take one step at a time. Start by breaking down the issue into smaller, more manageable pieces and focus on tackling one piece at a time. Identify any potential hindrances, and work to find solutions that can help you move forward.

If you're facing a difficult decision, take some time to consider all of your options, ask for advice from trusted sources, and weigh the pros and cons of each choice. Another important thing to remember is to stay positive.

It can be hard to remain optimistic when faced with an obstacle, but it is essential to stay focused on the end goal and keep a hopeful attitude throughout the process. Remind yourself of why you are trying to overcome the obstacle and how it will benefit you in the long run.

C. MAKING ADJUSTMENTS

Making adjustments is an important part of any process. Whether you are adjusting a machine, a recipe, or a plan, the goal is to ensure that the end result is as good as possible. When making adjustments, it's important to take into account the environment, the resources available, and the desired outcome.

It's also important to consider the cost and time involved in making adjustments. Start by analyzing the current situation, and then decide what needs to be changed. Make sure the changes you make are feasible and will not cause further problems. It's also important to test any changes you make to ensure that they are effective. You may need to make several adjustments before you find the best solution.

Finally, make sure that you document all adjustments you make. This will ensure that you can recreate the process if needed, and it will help you identify any problems that may arise in the future.

IV . BENEFITS OF ACHIEVING

Goals Achieving goals is essential to living a fulfilling life. It can help you stay motivated, focused, and productive, while also helping you to develop skills and qualities that will serve you well in all areas of life. Here are some of the key benefits of achieving goals:

1. Improved Self-Confidence: When you set goals and achieve them, you can feel proud of your accomplishments. This can help you to develop a stronger sense of confidence and self-esteem, which can be beneficial in all areas of life.

2. Improved Focus: Setting and achieving goals can help to keep your focus on the things that are most important to you. This can help you to stay organized and productive, and to prioritize tasks more effectively.

3. Improved Time Management: Achieving goals can help to improve your time management skills. By setting goals and deadlines, you can better manage your time and work on tasks more efficiently.

4. Increased Motivation: Accomplishing goals can give you a sense of satisfaction and achievement. This can help to increase your motivation and drive to keep pushing forward and working on other goals.

5. Improved Problem-Solving Skills: Achieving goals can help you to develop problem-solving skills as you will be forced to come up with creative solutions to any problems that arise along the way.

6. Improved Self-Discipline: Achieving goals can help you to become more disciplined and focused. You will be able to better control your thoughts and actions, and stay on the path to success.

7. Improved Mental Health: Achieving goals can help to improve your mental health. You will have a sense of purpose and direction, which can help to reduce stress and anxiety. Overall, achieving goals can help to improve your quality of life and make you a more successful and productive person. So, if you haven't already, start setting goals and start achieving them today!

A. BOOSTING SELF-CONFIDENCE

Self-confidence is the belief in oneself and one's abilities. It is an important factor in achieving personal and professional success. Boosting one's self-confidence can be achieved through a variety of methods, including positive self-talk, self-care, setting achievable goals, and taking risks. Positive self-talk is the practice of speaking kindly to oneself.

It is important to remember that one's thoughts affect behavior, so it is important to make sure that one's inner dialogue is positive and encouraging. This can be accomplished by replacing negative thoughts with positive ones and by focusing on one's strengths and accomplishments. Self-care is an important part of boosting self-confidence.

Taking time to relax, practice mindfulness, and engage in activities that bring joy can help to reduce stress and increase feelings of self-worth. Setting achievable goals can also be a great way to boost self-confidence. Goals should be specific, measurable, attainable, and realistic. Taking the time to break down goals into smaller, more manageable tasks can help to ensure that they are attainable.

Boosting self-confidence can be accomplished through a variety of methods.

It is important to remember that self-confidence is a journey and that it takes time and effort to build up. With the right tools, anyone can become more confident and capable.

B. ENHANCING QUALITY OF LIFE

Improving the quality of life requires taking the necessary steps to ensure the physical, mental and emotional well-being of individuals. Quality of life can be enhanced through a variety of actions, ranging from making healthy lifestyle choices to engaging in meaningful activities.

1. Make Healthy Choices: Eating a nutritious diet, exercising regularly, and getting adequate sleep are essential for maintaining physical and mental health. Choosing fresh, whole foods, engaging in physical activity, and maintaining regular sleep patterns are key for improving quality of life.

2. Engage in Meaningful Activities: Pursuing activities that bring pleasure and fulfillment can help to improve quality of life. Participating in hobbies, volunteering, or engaging in activities with friends and family are all ways to inject meaning and joy into life.

3. Connect with Others: Building strong relationships with family, friends, and community members is essential for

improving quality of life. Connecting with others can help to reduce stress, boost self-esteem, and create a sense of belonging.

4. Practice Self-Care: Taking time each day to focus on self-care is important for enhancing quality of life. This could include getting a massage, listening to music, or taking a relaxing bath. Practicing self-care is essential for maintaining balance in life.

5. Disconnect from Technology: Taking time away from technology can help to reduce stress, boost mood, and improve quality of life. Taking regular breaks from screens can help to clear the mind and allow for more meaningful connections with others.

By taking steps to make healthy choices, engaging in meaningful activities, connecting with others, practicing self-care, and disconnecting from technology, individuals can enhance the quality of their lives.

V. ACHIEVING LASTING SUCCESS

Achieving lasting success is a process that takes time and dedication. It requires setting goals and creating a plan to achieve them, striving to stay focused and motivated, and persevering even when the going gets tough. Here are some tips to help you achieve lasting success:

1. Set SMART Goals: Setting specific, measurable, achievable, realistic, and timely (SMART) goals is a great way to stay focused and motivated. A SMART goal will help you stay on track and make sure that you don't get sidetracked.

2. Develop a Positive Mindset: Having a positive attitude is essential for achieving lasting success. Remind yourself that you can succeed and keep a positive outlook, even when things don't go your way.

3. Take Action: Taking action is the only way to make progress. Don't wait for the perfect opportunity; take initiative and make it happen.

4. Monitor Your Progress: Keeping track of your progress is a great way to stay motivated and celebrate your successes. 5. Stay Focused: It's easy to get sidetracked, but staying focused on your goals is key to achieving lasting success.

6. Persevere: Don't give up when the going gets tough. Persevere and remember why you're working towards your goals in the first place.

7. Celebrate Your Successes: Don't forget to take a moment to celebrate your successes. Acknowledge your accomplishments, no matter how small they may be. These tips will help you achieve lasting success.
Remember, success doesn't happen overnight. It takes hard work and dedication. With the right mindset and dedication, you can achieve your goals and reach true success.

VI. CONCLUSION

Dreams to Reality: Turning Aspirations into Achievements, A Practical Guide to Transforming Dreams into Tangible Reality" has provided readers with insight into the essential elements of success, from goal setting to creating an action plan to developing self-discipline.

Armed with the information provided in this book, readers can craft their own path to success and start making progress towards their goals. With the right strategies, consistent effort, and dedication, readers can unlock the secrets of achieving their goals and find the success they seek.